ABOVE: *Women employed as temporary farmworkers during the First World War. While three of them wear the traditional countrywoman's sunbonnet, their other clothes—long skirts, blouses and cardigans—would have been equally suitable for office work, worn with lighter-weight shoes but without the all-enveloping white aprons.*

COVER: *A detail from St James's Fair by Samuel Colman, reproduced by courtesy of the Curator, the City of Bristol Museum and Art Gallery.*

OCCUPATIONAL COSTUME and working clothes, 1776-1976

Avril Lansdell

Shire Publications Ltd

CONTENTS

First published 1977, reprinted 1984. Shire Album 27. ISBN 0 85263 383 1.

Printed in Great Britain by C. I. Thomas and Sons (Haverfordwest) Ltd, Press Buildings, Merlins Bridge, Haverfordwest, Dyfed.

ACKNOWLEDGEMENTS

The author is pleased to record her thanks to her husband, Mr H. W. Lansdell, for printing photographs from his own and the Weybridge Museum collections and to Mrs Marion Van der Voort for her general encouragement and help in typing the text. Among many others in museums, libraries, businesses and authorities special thanks are due to Dr Sadie Ward, of the Museum of English Rural Life, Reading University, and Mr Philip Daniell of the British Waterways Board.

Photographs and other illustrations are acknowledged as follows: Milk Marketing Board, page 16; British Waterways Board, pages 5 (left), 6 (right), 21 (right); Central Electricity Generating Board, page 7 (bottom); Chertsey Museum, pages 3, 24 (both); Hereford Public Library (through the Museum of English Rural Life), pages 8 (right), 12 (top right and bottom left); Felix Holling, Guildford Museum, page 14 (bottom); photograph by H. W. Lansdell, pages 5 (right), 15 (bottom), 19 (bottom right), 25 (top), 28 (bottom right); Luton Museum and Art Gallery, page 8 (left); photograph by courtesy of the Manx Museum, page 19 (top); Museum of English Rural Life, Reading, pages 1, 6 (left), 11 (all), 13 (both), 14 (top), 17, 20 (top left), 22 (right) and 23 (top right and bottom left); Museum of London, pages 4 (left), 28 (bottom left), 30 (top left); National Museum of Wales, page 20 (top right); John E. Ray Collection, East Sussex County Library, page 18 (left); Shell Photographic Library, page 21 (left); Robert Shopland, Waterway Productions Ltd, page 9 (right); C. F. F. Snow, pages 22 (left), 23 (bottom right); Society of Antiquaries, Newcastle-upon-Tyne (through Northumberland County Record Office), page 19 (bottom left); Waterways Museum, page 31 (left); Welsh Folk Museum, page 20 (bottom); Weybridge Museum, pages 4 (right), 7 (top), 9 (left), 10 (both), 26 (right), 27 (both), 29 (top), 30 (top right and bottom); C. G. Williams Ltd, page 12 (bottom right); by courtesy of Mrs R. Vaughan Williams, page 18 (right); John Wisden & Co. Ltd, page 25 (bottom); author's collection, pages 26 (left), 28 (top); sketch by author, page 29 (bottom); from W. H. Pyne's *Microcosm,* pages 12 (top left), 23 (top left); from Stephens's *Book of the Farm,* page 15 (top). Cover illustration from 'St James's Fair' by Samuel Colman, reproduced by courtesy of the City of Bristol Museum and Art Gallery.

Men in the workshop of Lang's Propeller Works, Weybridge, c.1914. They wear basic working clothes with carpenters' aprons.

INTRODUCTION

Everyone likes to watch other people at work, and we all have a mental picture of different kinds of people at work. The clothes they wear are part of this picture and we become accustomed to them from childhood, for there are many children's books depicting the striped apron of the milkman, the gumboots of the farmer and the overalls of the garage mechanic. Occupational symbols in the clothes of those carrying out their daily work are part of the visual world about us and become so familiar that we do not even think about them. Yet we would miss them if they were swept away in favour of an undistinguished single uniform garment, or think it very odd if we saw a man baking bread in the oilskins of a deep-sea fisherman, or a farm tractor-driver wearing the bowler hat, pinstriped suit and lightweight shoes we associate with a present-day city businessman.

Many books have been written about the history of fashionable costume and many museums have collections of such clothes. There are far fewer books about working clothes and only a few examples shown in museums. Yet working clothes are, at any one time, very varied; they, too, have had their fashions, sometimes in step with fashionable clothes, often lagging behind them, and occasionally even influencing them.

Some occupations now include a uniform to make the wearers instantly recognisable. These jobs, among them the police, postmen and firemen, are not included here. This book describes basic working clothes over the past two hundred years, together with their variations and the different types of aprons, overalls and accessories worn on top of those basic clothes which make them 'occupational costume'.

ABOVE LEFT: *The drover. Painted in 1808. He wears breeches buttoned at the knee over striped stockings, neat shoes and short spats. Under his white jacket he would have worn a shirt and a waistcoat. He also wears a neckerchief and a soft hat. His drover's licence is fastened to his left arm.*

ABOVE RIGHT: *Workers at a cooperage in Hersham, Surrey, in the 1870s. The man on the left wears trousers and jacket covered by a long cloth apron. The man on the right is wearing an apron made from a piece of leather doubled over a belt. The top edge is hidden by his waistcoat and under it he wears dark trousers and a striped shirt. The man in the centre wears white trousers and a white Surrey 'slop' jacket. All three men wear hats, not unusual in a workshop where sawdust, smoke or dust are common.*

BASIC WORKING CLOTHES: MEN

In the late eighteenth century the clothes of the average working man consisted of a wide-cut shirt, breeches, stockings, sometimes with gaiters over them, a hat and a waistcoat. Over these he could wear a jacket or a greatcoat. Sometimes a greatcoat indicated a calling such as a watchman or a coachman. For extra warmth these coats had big collars and shoulder capes. For ease of movement most men discarded coats and jackets while at work and wore their waistcoats unbuttoned. For very strenuous work they sometimes left off their waistcoats but seldom left off their shirts. A shirt was an undergarment and was often used as nightwear as well.

Only sailors and very poor shepherds wore long trousers. All other men wore breeches fastening below the knee with buttons, buckles or tapes. However, long trousers were worn by middle-class small boys. In 1807 the Prince of Wales, later the Prince Regent, wore a pair of sailor's white duck trousers while on holiday at Brighton; within thirty years long trousers had replaced knee breeches for most social classes. The exceptions were court dress and men working with horses. Some elderly workmen continued to wear breeches to the 1840s.

Trousers were cut, as breeches had been, with a front flap, fastened at each side of the waist. Fly fronts were fashionable from the late 1830s but working trousers were made with front falls until the end of the century.

Long trouser ends tended to drag round the ankles and many men tied a string or hay-twist round the trousers just below the knee. This string had a variety of names, among them *yorks, lijahs, bowy-yanks* and *whirlers*. These names can be traced back to dialect words meaning leggings or gaiters.

By the mid nineteenth century the working man wore his trousers with a collarless shirt topped by a waistcoat and a coloured handkerchief round his neck. Although basic clothes remained unchanged, hats altered frequently. In Regency times farmers and gardeners wore a form of top hat; other workers wore soft felt hats with varying crowns and brims. By the 1850s farmworkers wore billycock hats and gardeners wore bowlers. Bowlers came to be worn by foremen among

BELOW LEFT: *A Victorian employee of the Weaver Navigation Company clears snow in 1895, wearing dark trousers, waistcoat and striped shirt. Even in summer he would have worn the same clothes.*

BELOW RIGHT: *His counterparts in 1975, working in a drained canal lock chamber, are stripped down to jeans and wellingtons. The man on the right also wears a coloured singlet with white edges.*

ABOVE LEFT: *In the first decade of the twentieth century a sweep from Bude, Cornwall, wears an early boiler suit in blue cotton. His flat cap is probably black or blue wool.*

ABOVE RIGHT: *'American-style' overalls were first advertised in 1905. They became very popular and are still worn today. This photograph shows carpenters at Norbury Junction Maintenance Yard, in 1962, wearing these bib and brace overalls with short-sleeved shirts and sleeveless pullovers.*

manual workers, by boatmen, by town clerks, and finally in the twentieth century by city businessmen.

In the mid nineteenth century many town workers and tradesmen wore square paper caps. These were replaced by peaked cloth caps towards the end of the century and cloth caps became almost universal among working men until the 1930s, since when young men have tended to abandon general headwear altogether for work. Only specialised 'occupational' hats, for example safety helmets or the hygienic white caps for bakers and cooks, are worn now.

Today many workers wear jeans, the blue canvas trousers first made for miners in the USA in the 1850s. In the 1920s white singlets began to replace Victorian long-sleeved undervests and are now available in bright colours and are worn with jeans as summer working garments.

Aprons of various shapes are worn over basic clothes as required. They vary in style and fabric as the work demands, unchanged in shape since the middle ages or earlier. The first overalls were the shepherds' and wagoners' smocks; the first dark coverall one-piece garments were worn by sweeps in the late nineteenth century. Bib and brace overalls were worn by many workers from the 1900s onward. Today many workers wear white coveralls, carrying the badge of their employers.

RIGHT: *A worker at the Urban Electricity Supply Company, Weybridge, stands before the distribution board, in 1913. He wears the clothes that were basic to all working men from about 1830 to 1945. As an indoor worker, however, he wears a collar and tie.*

BELOW: *After the Second World War waistcoats began to disappear, and overalls for neatness were adopted by many organisations for their workers. These men in white overalls are at the Bradwell nuclear power station in the 1960s.*

ABOVE LEFT: *An old lacemaker from the East Midlands in the mid nineteenth century wears a print dress, a small shawl and a large apron. She wears two caps, the inner one fastened beneath the chin in an eighteenth-century style. The top cap has her spectacles fastened to it. The style of her clothes spans two centuries and could have been worn by a working woman from 1820, or earlier, to 1914.*

ABOVE RIGHT: *A Hereford field worker in the 1890s on her way to work in the hop fields. She wears an ankle-length dress covered by a long white apron and a check shawl. On her head she wears the countrywoman's sunbonnet so common between 1840 and 1914.*

BASIC WORKING CLOTHES: WOMEN

Eighteenth-century working women wore a shift, an ankle-length petticoat with a pair of leather stays and a bibless apron. Over this they wore a low-necked gown, revealing the edge of the shift at the neck and sleeve ends. To fill in the bare neck they added a large kerchief round their shoulders, the point hanging down the back and the ends tucked into their gown. The front of the overskirt was often tucked up at the waist to reveal the shorter petticoat.

Although fashionable costume underwent a great many changes between 1776 and 1830, the working women continued to wear this basic costume. By the 1820s fashionable costume ceased to be based on a single high-waisted muslin garment, and working women began to wear simplified fashionable styles usually just after they had gone out of fashion. This could be accounted for by the vast trade in used clothes which were stripped of their trimmings and could be third- and fourth-hand, having been passed on from mistress to servant before coming on the market. New clothes were made in simplified versions of these just passed fashions by town women, and only in rural areas did the petticoat, shift, stays and handkerchief continue until the middle of the century.

Aprons were essential and two at a time were commonplace. A working woman felt undressed without an apron, indoors or out, and they were worn by field workers, street vendors and on canal boats as well as by indoor workers in all occupations. Some outdoor workers wore them hitched up on one side.

Out-of-doors eighteenth-century women had worn small caps with straw hats over them. The cap was also always worn indoors. By the middle of the nineteenth century the country woman had replaced cap and straw hat with the sunbonnet, a distinctively English rural headdress with a stiffened brim, lines of ruching and cording across the crown, and a frill, or *curtain,* over the neck and shoulders. The most elaborate bonnets were worn by the boatwomen. Sunbonnets gave good protection against sun, wind and, to some extent, rain. Sunburn was a disgrace, and even farm women took steps to avoid it. While fashionable women went bareheaded indoors, working women covered their hair until the twentieth century; even little girls wore caps and sunbonnets.

They were less concerned about revealing their ankles, or even legs, for working women's skirts were usually much shorter than fashionable ones, showing stout shoes or boots. Fisher girls would turn their skirts up to the knee. Working women's skirts were often edged and decorated with bands of contrasting colours or rows of deep tucks above the hem.

Towards the end of the nineteenth

BELOW LEFT: *By the early years of this century caps and bonnets began to disappear. This washerwoman could have come from any town in England. She wears a serge skirt folded over to reveal a waterproofed cotton lining. Her petticoat thus serves as an apron. Over her cotton blouse she has a neckerchief which she can use as a headscarf when she goes out.*
BELOW RIGHT: *From the late 1920s many working women wore cross-over flowered overalls on top of ordinary clothes (see also bottom left picture, page 12). This boatwoman, photographed on board the 'Keppel' on the Trent and Mersey Canal, was still wearing such an overall in 1959.*

century the distinctive dresses of country and town workers began to die out. Most women wore as fashionable a bodice as they could, even with a plain gathered skirt. Bustles were contrived from pads of old cloth; although they never reached the proportions of fashionable clothes they were worn well into the 1890s by country women. Late nineteenth-century aprons had bibs with wide straps over the shoulders. Indoor workers added frills to these straps, but many outdoor workers still wore bibless waist aprons. In the twentieth century, over short skirts, a wrapper-like sleeveless overall made of flowered cotton became common wear. They are now associated with women cleaners though at one time they replaced aprons even for outdoor workers.

Although trousers had been worn in mines by women in the early nineteenth century they were rare above ground. By the 1890s some old women farmworkers occasionally wore trousers. Only in the First World War did they become common, worn with knee-length overalls by land girls and munition workers. Working women returned to skirts, much shorter than before, between the wars, but revived trousers in 1939. Today trousers or jeans are common working wear for many women.

ABOVE: *By 1900 farm women near towns had abandoned the country sun-bonnet in favour of large hats. These seasonal workers at Hersham, Surrey, helped harvest vegetables.*
BELOW: *A girl at Bell Farm, Hersham, in 1944 wears the bib and brace overalls issued to the war-time Women's Land Army for use when their regular uniform of breeches and jumper was too hot. These 'dungarees' were also worn by school-girl casual workers during summer holiday employment.*

ABOVE LEFT: *This ploughman (1801) wears a plain, short smock, swathed round his waist, over breeches, stockings, ankle boots, shirt, waistcoat and a neckerchief.*

ABOVE RIGHT: *A Hereford labourer c. 1900 uses a bagging hook. He wears white corduroy trousers, with straps round the knee, a shirt, neckerchief and a waistcoat with slit sides. Because his job involves bending a smock would get in his way.*

WORKERS ON THE LAND

Farmworkers wore clothes that gave warmth, ease of movement and protection from the weather. Like other working men, once breeches and gaiters disappeared, they tied straps round their trousers below the knee, but the distinctive English garment associated with farmworkers is the smock. Made in white, grey, fawn, blue or green linen in different parts of the country, it indicated occupation by the length and its district of origin by its cut. Eighteenth-century smocks were plain until its last quarter when the first honeycombing is recorded. The embroidered motives were nineteenth-century and did not necessarily symbolise the wearer's work. Nor were smocks always worn; there were many farm jobs where a smock would have got in the way.

RIGHT: *An assistant at the Museum of English Rural Life, Reading, demonstrates a seed fiddle; he is wearing a late nineteenth-century smock and trouser strings over modern jeans. The photograph looks 'wrong' because he is not wearing a hat.*

ABOVE: *Early nineteenth-century hop-pickers wear basic working dress with aprons and mob caps. One woman wears a hat over her cap.*

ABOVE RIGHT: *Casual farmworkers and hop-pickers have always worn current working-class fashion. This woman wears a straw boater, and a fringed shawl over her long skirt and big apron. The foreman wears his string of 'tallies' over his shoulder. Hereford, 1900.*

BELOW LEFT: *Hop-pickers in Hereford, 1937. The man wears a shirt, neck scarf and waistcoat with a knitted cardigan over it. All three men in these pictures wear flat, peaked caps, almost unchanged in sixty years. This woman wears the typical 1930s flowered sleeveless overall with a dress and hat.*

BELOW RIGHT: *A hop-picker in Kent in 1966 wears a fashionable mini-skirt covered with a short apron. She does not wear a hat. The man behind her, of an older generation, wears a cap, a shirt and a pullover, probably over grey flannel trousers.*

ABOVE LEFT: *A hedger in Hereford in the 1890s turns a sack into a smock. He wears heavy mittens and a light-coloured felt hat over basic working clothes with trouser straps.*

ABOVE RIGHT: *Twenty years later, c. 1910-14, another Hereford hedger wears corduroy trousers and a waistcoat with a collar. Although this photograph was obviously taken in better weather than the one to the left he still wears a cap on his head and carries his leather mittens.*

FENCING AND HEDGING

English farmworkers have worn gloves or mittens for work, where possible, since the middle ages. The most common were the leather mittens used by hedgers, whose work involved handling thorny branches. To protect their clothes hedgers also have worn smocks or aprons made of coarse sacking. These sacking garments give additional warmth, for hedging is often done in weather unsuited to other farm work. Modern farmworkers have been known to wear heavy-quality polythene fertiliser sacks for the same purpose.

SHEPHERDS

Although smocks were worn by many farm labourers they have come to be associated with shepherds, who wore their smocks long enough to cover their knees. A smock made of thick linen, closely gathered with smocking stitch, with a large cape collar, would be both warm and fairly waterproof. Extra garments could be worn beneath it, for a smock was always a full, loose garment.

The smocks from South Wales and the Hereford and Gloucestershire districts have a great deal of smocking and embroidery on them, as well as large collars which sometimes extend over the shoulders. Smocks from Surrey and Sussex seem to be of finer linen with a minimum of smocking and embroidery. Many smocks in museums are undocumented and as long smocks were worn by carters

as well as by shepherds, it is not always possible to tell who could have worn a particular smock.

SHEEP SHEARING

Sheep shearing demands strength, skill and a manner of handling animals that soothes rather than frightens. Some shepherds sheared their own sheep, but often the sheep shearer of the nineteenth century was an itinerant worker, moving from farm to farm at the appropriate time of the year.

No special clothing was worn, but the sheep-shearer needed freedom of movement in his clothes unless he was very skilled.

LEFT: *Shepherds wore their smocks over ordinary working clothes. This shepherd in 1900 carries his smock over his arm and wears a shirt, waistcoat, trousers with 'yarks', and two jackets. His hat is a soft felt.*

BELOW LEFT: *An eighteenth-century shepherd in an undecorated smock (from a painting by George Morland).*

BELOW RIGHT: *Sketches of two smock types from Guildford Museum. The top smock is the typical Surrey and Sussex smock with very little gathering and embroidery. The bottom smock is typical of the South Midlands.*

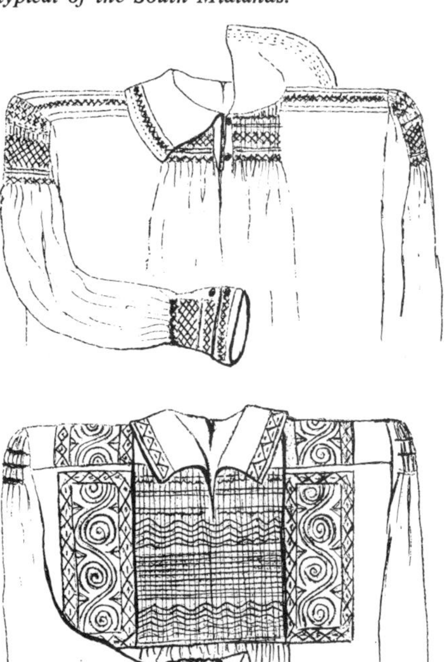

ABOVE: *This early Victorian sheep shearer has discarded his waistcoat and turned his braces off his shoulders to give him freedom of movement. Note the low-set sleeve in his shirt, which is cut like an undecorated smock or an eighteenth-century shirt.*

RIGHT: *Photographed at a sheep-shearing competition in 1973, this Welsh farmer has put a brown button-through overall on top of his best town suit. Shearing sheep is not part of his daily work and only during a holiday competition in a nearby village can he show his skill at hand shearing. Nowadays sheep are sheared with electric clippers.*

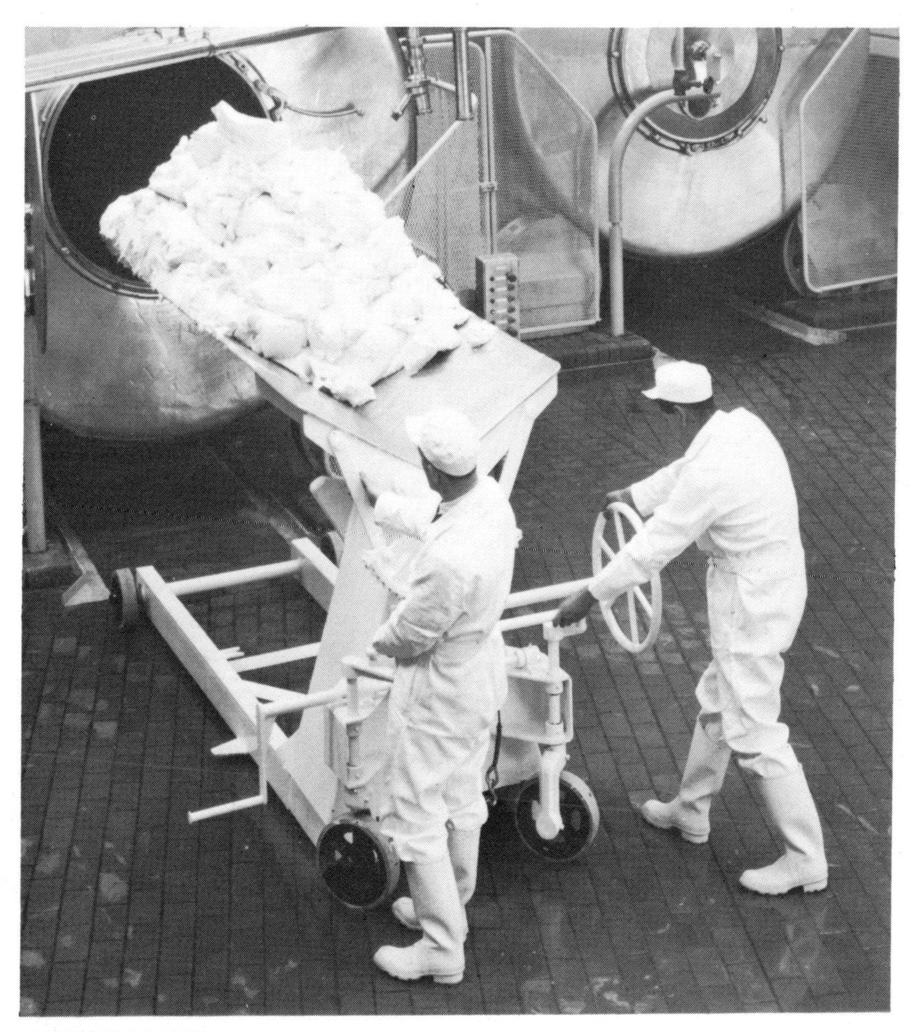

BUTTERMAKING

Until the First World War most butter was made in cottages or farmhouses by hand in wooden churns. Butter is still made in small quantities by similar methods in Welsh farmhouses, although the churn is as likely to be turned by a small electric motor as by hand.

The bulk of butter now sold commercially is made in huge stainless-steel churns in factory-like creameries where the operators wear special overalls to preserve the cleanliness of the product.

ABOVE: *Butter being taken from the churn at Kendal Creameries in the 1970s. Each churn can make two tons of butter in two and a half hours. The men wear white coveralls, white linen caps and white rubber boots.*

OPPOSITE: *A countrywoman churning butter in 1805. She wears a striped dress bunched up over a plain petticoat. Her neckerchief matches her dress and her large apron covers her from the waist down. She wears a small mob cap.*

ABOVE LEFT: *Hastings fishermen of the 1890s in canvas trousers and 'slops' worn over dark blue sweaters. They also wear 'sou'wester' oilskin hats.*

ABOVE RIGHT: *A Norfolk 'ganzey' with cable patterns only on the shoulders. These traditional patterns are related to the Aran and Guernsey sweaters with various symbolic designs.*

OPPOSITE TOP: *Kipper girls on the Isle of Man 'washing down' their black oilskin overskirts in the sea. Beneath their oilskins they wear short-sleeved, calf-length dresses and go barefoot.*

OPPOSITE BOTTOM LEFT: *This 1905 photograph of North Shields fish quay shows two Northumberland Cullercoats fishwives with their heavily tucked skirt. Fishwives' skirts, nearly always above the ankles, shocked Victorian travellers.*

OPPOSITE BOTTOM RIGHT: *A kipper girl, photographed at Peel, Isle of Man, in 1969, wears an overskirt in white oilskin, almost identical to those in the photograph above, over a sweater (sleeves rolled up to the elbows), jeans and wellington boots.*

WORKERS BY THE SEA

FISHERMEN AND FISHERWOMEN

Traditionally the clothes worn by fishermen have appeared very different to those worn by workers on the land. Yet they fulfil the same function and in many cases are the same shape as landsmen's clothes. The fisherman's overshirt, called a *slop,* is cut like a labourer's short smock but made of waterproof canvas with no decoration.

Some confusion has arisen in that the same name has been used for different garments. A slop can be a short white jacket worn by Surrey labourers (see page 4) or a fisherman's garment made of canvas or oilskin, or a sailor's very wide-cut breeches or trousers.

Slops worn in Norfolk and all along the east coast of Britain were usually blue for fishermen, crab and lobster men and whelk gatherers, except in Yarmouth, where the herring fishers wore brown slops. Brown slops were also worn by men from the fresh-water Broads and were equally worn on land or water. Early oilskin slops were black.

The clothes worn by the wives and daughters of fishermen have tended to be distinctive, especially in the North.

ABOVE LEFT: *A Whitstable shrimper in th 1920s wears a long black oilskin slop ove trousers shortened to above the ankle. H carries a pair of 'back-steynes', wide oversho to enable him to walk safely on soft sand.*

ABOVE RIGHT: *A mid Victorian girl, sellin prawns in Tenby, South Wales, wears a sho skirt over black shoes and stockings. He short-sleeved jacket shows the long sleeves her blouse. To protect her clothes she wears black apron and a little red shawl. On her hea she wears a frilled white cap fastened beneat the chin, with a little black hat on top, also he by a band under her chin.*

LEFT: *A modern cockle gatherer from Sout Wales.*

ABOVE LEFT: *A North Sea oil diver adjusting his aqualung while dressing for duty. He still has to finish fastening his wet-suit and add flippers and face-mask to his equipment before being ready to dive.*

ABOVE RIGHT: *A diver working in the Caledonian Canal in 1957, about to receive his helmet. Beneath his diving suit he wears a woollen sweater, trousers and probably long underwear. On his head is a woollen cap, worn both to protect his head from the helmet and for warmth.*

THE DIVERS

The occupational costume that above all others indicates the wearer's work is the diving suit. The first diving suits were heavy and cumbersome rubber suits with lead-soled shoes and huge metal shoulder yokes and helmets. Descents in diving suits were first made in 1837, and ever since then attempts have been made to lighten the suit and simplify the equipment, thus making it possible to perform many tasks under water. The modern development whereby a diver carries his own air supply with him makes for the efficiency of the skin-diver in his rubber wet suit and flippers.

ABOVE LEFT: *A thatcher in Essex in 1941 wears 'leathers' made of sacking wound round his knees.*

ABOVE RIGHT: *Resting on the ground a thatcher from Kilkhampton, North Cornwall, in 1902, shows off his leather knee-pads and the palm on his right hand.*

RURAL CRAFTS

THATCHING

Since the materials (straw or reed) used by the thatcher are tough, springy and spiky he needs protection in his clothes, and usually he wore clothes of strong material; canvas, corduroy or moleskin trousers had pads, usually of leather, strapped to the knees. These pads were always called *leathers,* even when made of sacking. A thatcher could also wear a leather *palm,* or metal or leather *thimbles* on his fingers.

BRICKMAKERS

Early brickmaking was a family craft, both women and children digging clay, pugging and working it, and shaping the bricks. The work was heavy and arduous. Eighteenth-century brickmaking families often lived in out-of-doors squalor, bare-foot and poverty-stricken. With the nineteenth-century building booms the trade became more organised, but quite small children were employed in brick-yards to fetch and to carry until 1872, when an Act was passed prohibiting child labour in brickyards.

From then on brickmaking became men's work. Large country estates had their own brickyards, where bricks were made by the estate staff and then fired by itinerant brickburners. Brickmakers generally wore the ordinary working clothes with the addition of canvas and leather aprons.

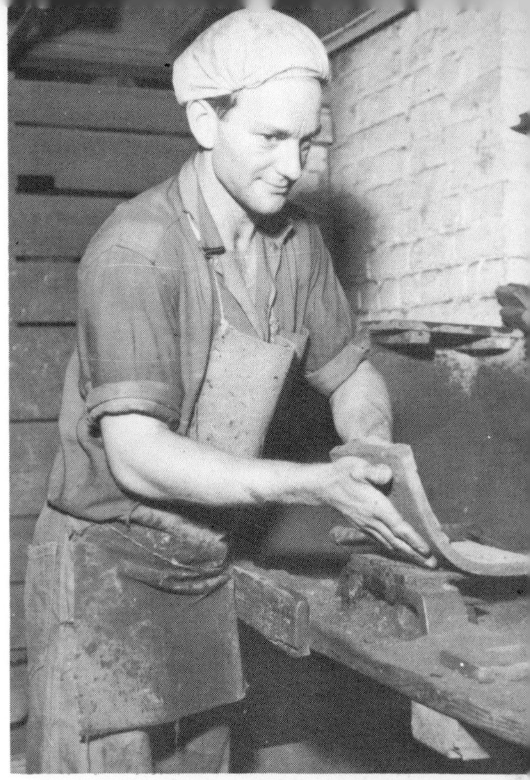

ABOVE: *Early nineteenth-century barefoot brickmakers. The women and children wear basic working clothes. The men wear belted leather jerkins instead of the normal waistcoats.*

RIGHT AND BELOW: *Brick and tile makers photographed in the early 1930s and 1940s. Note the knotted handkerchief worn on the head of the tile-former, the leather aprons and the hand protector known as a 'cott'. This was of leather or canvas, but by the 1950s cotts were often cut out of an old rubber inner tube.*

ABOVE: *These blacksmiths at Ottershaw, Surrey, in 1900, wore basic working clothes with leather aprons. It is significant that the man on the left feels free to wear no waistcoat and works in his shirt and braces. Both smiths wear leather aprons held in place with wide leather belts. Blacksmiths' aprons were often fringed or split at the bottom. The younger smith in this picture has an apron split up the centre so that it covers each leg separately. The man leading the horse wears straps both above and below his knees. All three wear caps.*

LEFT: *Another blacksmith, also at Ottershaw, shows off his split apron. His clothes are virtually unchanged from the previous generation; this photograph was taken in 1936.*

LEATHER WORKERS

The protective clothing worn by shoemakers, repairers and other workers in leather, such as cricket-ball makers and saddlers, has changed little over the years. A leather apron has proved the most effective, although Weybridge Museum has a shoe repairer's cloth apron which was worn with a leather chest bib. Protection for the hands when sewing leather was given by a palm protector, or *hand-leather,* a strip of leather worn round the hand, not covering the fingers, which took the pull of the waxed thread.

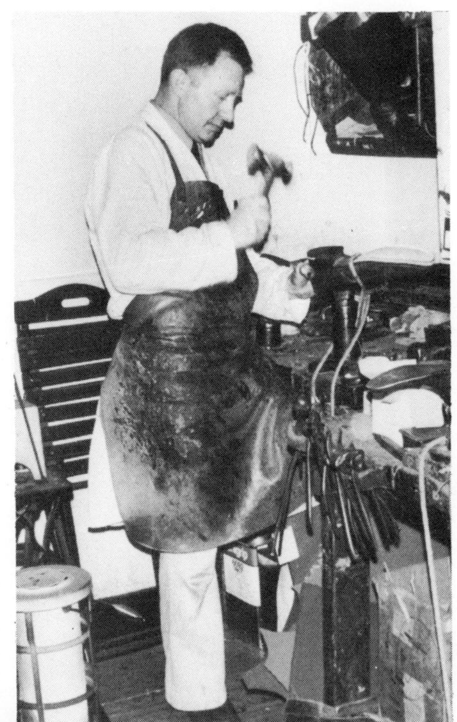

RIGHT: *A shoe-repairer, photographed in 1976, wears a leather apron over a white overall. Beneath this he wears a shirt and tie and light blue jeans.*

BELOW: *A craftsman stitching the four quarters of a cricket ball together wears a canvas and leather apron over shirt, trousers and waistcoat. Note the 'hand-leather' protecting his left hand.*

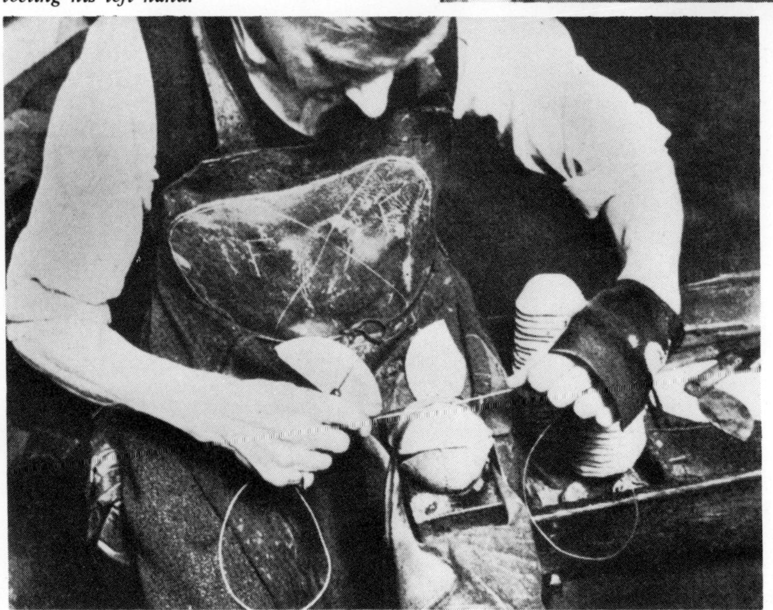

LEFT: *A Victorian picture shows the family gardener in his light-coloured trousers and collared waistcoat, leather gaiters and bowler hat. The apron was normally of blue canvas and this man wore it doubled over a belt.*

BELOW: *A municipal gardener lifting fuchsias, wearing trousers, wellington boots and a sleeveless sheepskin jerkin worn over his jacket.*

GARDENERS

In the past all big houses had a team of gardeners. Most of them loved their work and, starting as boys, grew old in the service of one or two gardens. They were trusted servants and were often the confidants of the young people of the house. Their successors are the gardeners employed by municipal councils who keep the parks and public gardens a delight to the eye. The traditional blue apron is now usually only worn for greenhouse work.

TRADESMEN

ABOVE: *Two butchers from Esher, Surrey, in the 1890s. The man on the left wears a high-buttoned single-breasted blue or grey overall and a narrow-striped blue and white apron with its top edge turned down at the waist. The man on the right wears a darker blue roll-collared overall, a white apron buttoned to this at the top, and a blue and white apron over this. Butchers generally referred to their overalls as smocks, even though, by the late nineteenth century, they no longer resembled the smock worn by shepherds or farm labourers (see page 14).*

RIGHT: *The fishmonger of Weybridge, c. 1900, wore knickerbockers and heavy socks beneath a blue overall and oilskin apron. Other fishmongers wore gaiters or tucked the ends of their trousers in their boots. On his arms the fishmonger wore white oversleeves to protect the cuffs of his shirt and overall. Like his apron they were probably waterproof.*

BERRYLAND

JMO 757B

ABOVE: *The staff of a late Victorian bakery line up with the owner and his dog. They are dressed in an assortment of aprons and overalls worn over basic working clothes. Note the man on the left in a dark apron. He may have been responsible for tending the fires and the ovens. Note, too, the way the man on the right has rolled his apron round his waist, showing the points of his waistcoat below it.*

BELOW: *Workers in a bakery in the 1970s wear specially designed white cotton or linen trousers, shirts and caps. The supervisor wears dark trousers under his overall. He still retains the tradition of wearing a different style of hat, although it is no longer a bowler.*

OPPOSITE TOP: *The young man and the boy, delivering milk in Surbiton in 1913, are both wearing trousers, boots and gaiters. The boy wears a high-buttoned jacket and an Eton collar. The young man wears a stiff collar and tie, with a scarf tucked round his neck below his waistcoat. This and his jacket may belong to a 'best suit', now demoted to working clothes. Despite the dark linen apron and money bag he is something of a dandy with a bowler hat and watch and chain.*

OPPOSITE BOTTOM LEFT: *A milk girl of 1808 wears an ankle-length petticoat under a bunched-up dress. Her sleeves are rolled to the elbow showing the short sleeves of her undergarment. She wears a big neckerchief to protect her neck and shoulders from the yoke with which she carries her buckets of milk. A long apron is tied round her waist and she wears a straw hat over a little white cap.*

OPPOSITE BOTTOM RIGHT: *Although milkmen have worn blue and white striped aprons for over fifty years they are beginning to disappear and many milkmen today wear a short nylon overall coat. This milkman (1976) is a mixture of old and new, for he still wears a striped apron but tops it with the new overall.*

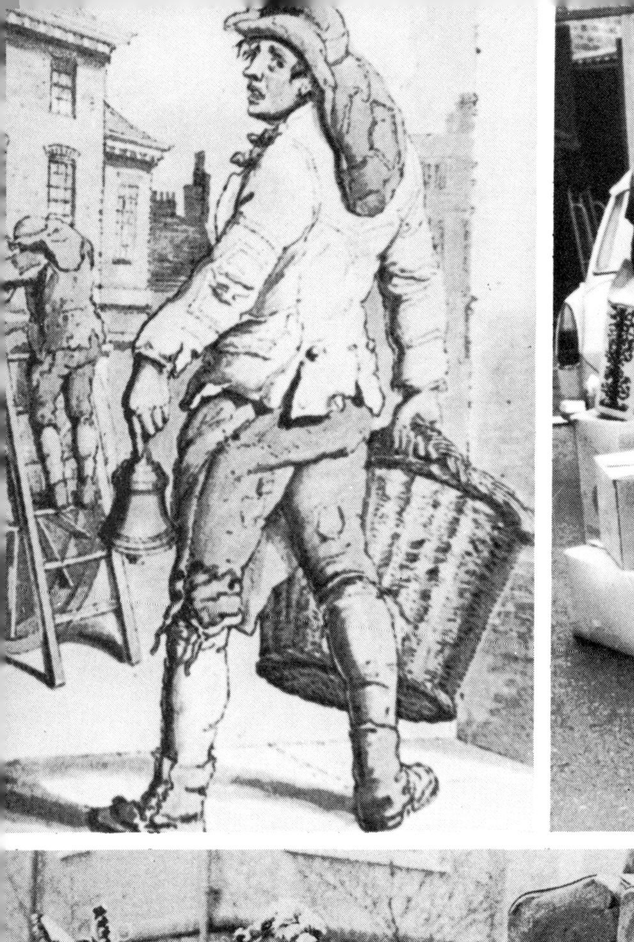

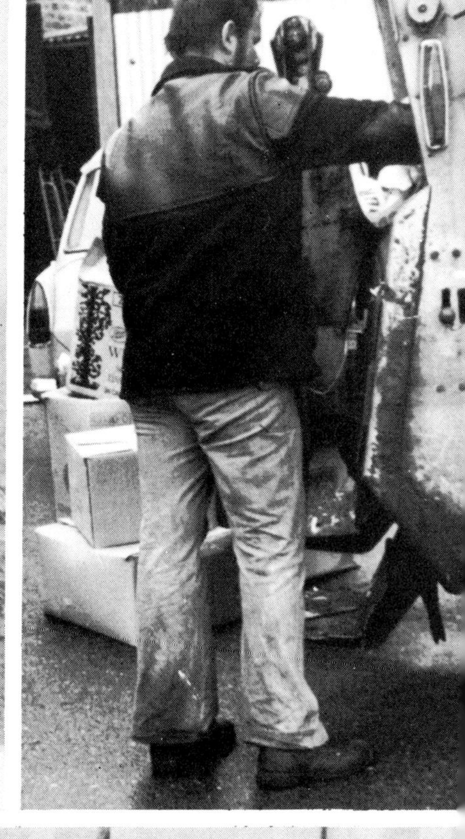

ABOVE LEFT: *A boatman's family c. 1900. The mother wears the distinctive boatwoman's clothes of skirt (covered by a large white apron), blouse, shoulder shawl and elaborate bonnet. It is similar to the farmwoman's bonnet but more elaborate. From 1901 their bonnets were usually black.*

ABOVE RIGHT: *Boatmen in moleskin or corduroy trousers, shirts, broad belts and braces and velvet caps. One wears a velvet waistcoat and an upstanding collar.*

THE CANALS

The inland waterways were a viable form of transport for nearly two hundred years, even though for over half the time they fought a steadily losing battle with the need for greater speed in transport. From about 1830 to 1840 onward it became common for the families of the boatmen to live on the narrowboats that originated on the Midland canals; to some extent they then lived in isolation from the villages through which they passed and so formed their own nomadic communities with distinctive clothes and traditions. Commercial carrying on the canals has declined rapidly during the past twenty years and the canals are now almost exclusively used by pleasure craft.

OPPOSITE TOP LEFT: *The London dustman in 1808 wears similar clothes to the drover (see page 4) with the addition of a short apron, tucked below his jacket, and a fan-tailed hat. This protected his neck and shoulders from the wear of the basket when hoisted on his shoulders or head.*

OPPOSITE TOP RIGHT: *The 1976 dustman still needs protection for his shoulders and this is given by leather panels in the back and shoulders of his jacket. Beneath this he wears a shirt and tough denim jeans.*

OPPOSITE BOTTOM: *The Victorian dustmen wear aprons made of sacking or canvas and collect rubbish in a cart little different to that used in 1808. The fan-tailed hat is replaced with a soft felt hat and a sacking shoulder cape. The chief dustman wears a bowler hat and the supervisor a flat cap, a leather collared jacket and leather gaiters over his trousers and boots.*

FURTHER READING

Anthony, Ilid. *The Countrymen's Smocks in the Welsh Folk Museum.* National Museum of Wales. 1974.
Cunnington, Phyllis, and Lucas, Catherine. *Occupational Costume in England.* A. & C. Black. 1967.
Hall, Maggie. *Smocks.* Shire Publications. 1979.
Harvey, M., and Compton, R. *Fisherman Knitting.* Shire Publications. 1978.
Johnstone White, William. *Working Class Costume.* Edited by Pamela Clabburn. Costume Society. 1973.
Lansdell, Avril. *The Clothes of the Cut.* British Waterways Board. 1975.
Lister, Margot. *Costume of Everyday Life.* Herbert Jenkins Ltd. 1972.
Oakes, Alma, and Hamilton-Hall, Margaret. *Rural Costume.* Batsford. 1970.
Pyne, W. H. *The Costumes of Great Britain.* 1808.
Pyne, W. H. *The Microcosm, Part I, Trades and Industries.* 1808-20. Reprinted Luton Museum, 1974.
Smart, John, and Griffiths, John. *Covering Up.* Science Museum. 1982.
Tarrant, Naomi. *Smocks in the Buckingham County Museum.* Buckingham County Council. 1976.
Thompson, Gladys. *Patterns of Guernseys, Jerseys and Arans — Fishermen's Sweaters from the British Isles.* Dover Paperbooks, 1971.
Various authors. *Strata of Society.* Papers of the Costume Society's Conference, Norwich, 1973.
Williams-Mitchell, Cristobel. *Dressed for the Job.* Blandford. 1982.

PLACES TO VISIT

Many museums have examples of occupational costume among collections of general clothes, but because few museums have complete outfits of working clothes they are not always on display. The most common item of occupational costume to be found in museums is the smock, and many provincial museums do display at least one smock. However, museum staff are usually willing to show costumes from their storerooms to interested visitors provided an appointment is made in advance.

Museums with occupational costume on show

Museum of English Rural Life, The University, Whiteknights, Reading, Berkshire RG6 2AG.Telephone: Reading (0734) 875123 extension 475.
The Science Museum, Exhibition Road, London SW7 2DD. Telephone: 01-589 3456.
Waterways Museum, Stoke Bruerne, Towcester, Northamptonshire. Telephone: Northampton (0604) 862229.

Other museums with occupational costume, some of which may be on show

Buckinghamshire County Museum, Church Street, Aylesbury, Buckinghamshire HP20 2QP. Telephone: Aylesbury (0296) 82158.
Cambridge and County Folk Museum, 2/3 Castle Street, Cambridge CB3 0AQ. Telephone: Cambridge (0223) 355159.
Colchester and Essex Museum, The Hollytrees, High Street, Colchester, Essex CO1 1TJ. Telephone: Colchester (0206) 76071.
Gallery of English Costume, Platt Fields, Rusholme, Manchester M14 5LL. Telephone: 061-224 5217.
Hereford and Worcester County Museum, Hartlebury Castle, near Kidderminster, Worcestershire DY11 7XZ. Telephone: Hartlebury (0299) 250416.
Laing Art Gallery, Higham Place, Newcastle upon Tyne, Tyne and Wear NE1 8AG. Telephone: Newcastle upon Tyne (0632) 327734.
Museum of Lakeland Life and Industry, Abbot Hall, Kendal, Cumbria LA9 5AL. Telephone: Kendal (0539) 22464.
Newark District Council Museum, Appletongate, Newark, Nottinghamshire NG24 1JY. Telephone: Newark (0636) 702358.
Oxfordshire County Museum, Fletcher's House, Woodstock, Oxfordshire OX7 1SN. Telephone: Woodstock (0993) 811456.
Rutland County Museum, Catmos Street, Oakham, Rutland, Leicestershire. Telephone: Oakham (0572) 3654.
Staffordshire County Museum, Shugborough, Stafford ST17 0XB. Telephone: Little Haywood (0889) 881388.
Strangers' Hall Museum, Charing Cross, Norwich, Norfolk NR2 4AL. Telephone: Norwich (0603) 611277.
Welsh Folk Museum, St Fagans, Cardiff, South Glamorgan CF5 6XB. Telephone: Cardiff (0222) 569441.